JN411152

Love and the Beginning

Love and the Beginning

A collection of new poems by Kwon Park
Translated by YoungShil Ji, Daniel T.Parker

K POET

아시아

Contents

LOVE AND THE BEGINNING

Assistance

I

will

love myself, rocks, valleys, glaciers, marmots, firm, deep, immense, in-betweens of palm trees and firs, not passive but firm, deep-deep, digging claws into immenseness, my decision is not to be happier but to be less unhappy, morality has a right to be merry, clearly no answer, nothing I can do, it has never been bright like this, never been, in the direction with light, in the light with direction, asking about someone is pure, pure footmarks, conviction of footsteps, conviction, resonance …

Assistance

I

will

get started, unlicensed nihility overflows, so constructive, isn't it? collapsing, collapsing, falling, skillfully safe, harmful effects? who cares? bullshit, construction, with no plausible reason, mobilize, forcefully mobilize, whence the source of driving force comes doesn't matter, special measures? well, they are makeshifts, somehow unobtrusively carve your flesh and build a runway of blood, a round of applause! cheer enthusiastically like a scorching summer, a round of watermelon is delicious, exactly so, how do powerful people always live so well? give up, I jump up, I come back home,

Assistance

I

will

get started, I should help me begin, if I don't help me who will? it's easier to carry a piece of blank paper when two people lift it, I should help, spring summer fall winter, I should live helping each self, a fake wall like a piece of blank paper, a fake wall like a piece of blank paper, a fake wall like a piece of blank paper, a fake wall like a piece of blank paper, each time, I execute an approach run, excessive sweat? other people have it too, I heard comparison helps our understanding, but why doesn't it give me any help? yet, I, help, me,

To Eat

Joon,

my mother's given name is Joon.

It's such a pretty-sounding name.

The fresh green of early summer.

Not like an old person's name.

Joon,

means "be a competent person,"

"be brilliant," or "pursue your goal"

in the Chinese alphabet,

why are the meanings such big deals?

Joon,

other meaning is "leftovers"

usually not used for names,

a family's desperate wish

for a son who can lead *jesa*.[1]

Joon,

this evening it is Joon again,

She will eat the old leftover rice.
Like a day commemorating the
ancestors. Like eating blessings to
descendants. She eats leftover rice.

Despite eating leftover rice, why
does she worry about being judged?

Yes, we used to eat food together,
we would drink alcohol together[2].

Gods, let us preserve our family,
Gods, give comfort to our family,

it was a matter of methods.
Leftover rice, she ate it alone, leftover rice, she chewed it well, leftover rice, she heated it up, leftover rice, she completely burned it, leftover rice, she put it into soup, leftover rice, she boiled it, leftover rice, she steamed it, leftover rice, she boiled it down, leftover rice, she scraped, licked her bowl, leftover rice, she never skipped a meal,

Eating finished?
Filming meokbang[3]?
deaf while eating?

I would have made her eat my words,
and I chew on that frame of mind.

In an English style garden,
a serpentine trail wanders,
as we stroll, stroll, and stroll,
a pond appears with cedars,
as we stroll, stroll, and stroll,
she's a subject to be cured.
As we stroll, stroll, and stroll,
naturally, formally,
monitored under control,
as we stroll, stroll, and stroll,

She goes to bed.
Leftovers go bad.

Translator's notes:

1 A memorial service to commemorate an ancestor's death day.

2 In South Korea, after holding the ritual of *jesa*, family members share food and drink.

3 An online eating show popular in South Korea.

Monday

Papayas, papayas, papayas, tropical nights,
papaya seeds, papaya seeds, planted in my head,
greenish-greenish-greenish-greenish-yellow-yellow,
papayas, papayas, growing for eternity
making their appearance, during the tropical nights,

You … I am, on the verge of, chronic fatigue syndrome

bright sunshine is bedazzling
just a typical summer
like a typical plant is

developing into green
then yellow finally gold

similar to God's image
it's similar to Monday
a no-meat-eating Monday

Tofu can imitate the special dish diners have when they shatter
the skull of a living monkey and pour hot oil inside it[1]

The shape of an animal
supremacy of tofu
the holy image of God

It's Monday, another Monday,
with torrential rain, pouring down,
resonating sound of rain, rain,

tenacious, inconsiderate,
the beginning of everything,

in the meanwhile

bright sunshine is bedazzling
in my head the papayas
are appearing appearing
summer of tropical nights
tropical nights of summer

Hey, today, with me, would you like to eat *som tam*[2] tossed with chopped fresh green papaya and a mixture of garlic and chili powder?

Poet's note:
1 *The Chinese Feast* (1995).

Translator's note:
2 A Thai-style green papaya salad.

Assurance

Hurrying. I was hurrying in the evening.
Hurrying during the morning too. Hurrying.
Catching my breath. I was hurrying. That day.
On that day. I was earnest. That is real love,
naturally, God? There is only one God.
It is undeniably clear on a Sunday.

Clear. The bag is clear. Sure? It is sure the bag doesn't have it. Clear. As for the bag it is clear. Love with soul is beautiful, love with faith is dangerous, love with a system is doubtful. He says. It is a bag. Is it? The security checkpoint agent suspects danger. A person who takes the first trip may feel only beautiful things. The suspicion of danger is not everything, but would you open your bag?

entire lamb's carcass barbecued
a piece of unleavened bread
offered on a special platter
and a goblet of fine red wine

With arms wide open I welcome
myself who does self-reflection
myself who is a warm person
you are clean and unpolluted
with arms wide open I welcome

You feel the pleasure
and are at peace like
the ruling classes
in a resort lodge?
Is today Sunday?

Over there, a dozen adult men,

Apple

One bad apple will spoil the entire bunch is the saying I
was always told.
So I'm fairly sure that I know what rotten things he has
stored in his cellar.

But I don't want to look at it.
The stairway catches cold and coughs,

pastel periwinkle spiral orchids are in terracotta pots in
the background,

I am being
dragged along the way

The bed is

on water

the sky and

the field are

earth-colored

He pounds nails into an apple

It's good for your health good for your health

The hovercraft he is carried in

is fully packed with uncountable

eels eels eels eels eels eels eels eels eels

It is overcooked

Chunky eel chowder

Now what should be done?

He pulls the nails out from the apple
It's good for your health good for your health

A snail with two horns
and chitinous teeth
that's why I like it
it curls in its shell
and slithers slowly
under the hot sun
melting like sliced cheese

It is good
having a dream about tiny worms crawling
having a dream where the tiny worms wriggle
Bonanza

A woman's history is just like an apple
he says that and makes an exact mold out of me
and stores the exact me copy in his cellar

Flies, the swarm of shining flies
are pretty
Tiny crystals of dark glass are
sparkling

dazzling

Friday

He married on Friday.
(His decision was economical and rational.)
On Saturday he went home.
(Suddenly thinking it was irrational,)
on Sunday he searched the Internet for "domestic violence without violence."
(Wishing it would be a rational decision this time ...)
On Monday he went to work.
(And that was a rational decision.)
On Tuesday he was demanded.
(Irrational.)
On Wednesday he was informed of a court decision.
(Unconditionally irrational.)
On Thursday he asked.
(How about Friday?)

The anniversary. Friday is the anniversary. Friday is the anniversary of God's suffering. Friday is the anniversary of God's suffering as you remember the meaning of sacrifice and love. Friday is the anniversary of God's suffering as you remember the meaning of sacrifice and love without eating anything. Friday is the anniversary of God's suffering as you remember the meaning of sacrifice and love without eating anything while restraining yourself. Commemorating is looking back. Does looking back mean commemorating? Are you commemorating? Are you looking back? If so today is Friday.

Plant

You look like a good person

The words you heard first the words you heard first today the words you heard first since last week the words you don't remember when was the last time you heard them

Once I asked

why you followed

you said you wanted to follow didn't care didn't at that moment you didn't

Why did you follow?

Why on earth?

I think I know why

I still think

the word good sounds
far
detached
It sounds like a religion that just spoke to me
or some types of plants for example

a foliage plant is exotic sunshine
an aquatic plant is someone who cries easily
a vine plant is very affable
a succulent plant is properly independent
a ground cover plant is hands held out when needed

A person who grows plants is a good person
I've heard that
In fact you wanted to look like a good person

Wanted to live well   So that was it

I just realized it

Most People

Most people completely ignore everything.

Victims make appeals to escape their torment,
but it is truly better to ignore them.
Sorry to say it, but that is for the best.

Do most people feel they are out of harm's way?

Obviously I'm not a perfect person.
In fact I may be the stupidest person,
and most people are the stupidest as well.

Are you a person who is like most people?

Do you follow the ways of most people?
Do you live in the spaces of most people?

Do you perceive the symbols of most people?

Gae-bae.

Gae-bae?

Gae-bae.

Did you say *bae-gae*[1] backward?

I mean "dawn."

Dawn?

Gae-bae in dialect from my parents' hometown means dawn.

It's hard to guess the meaning.

It sort of makes sense. It's like sleeping on a dawn, that kind of image?

You sound like a poet.

Poet?

I still don't know it, but I get it.

I don't know how people started to call the dawn *gae-bae*.

You were born in the countryside so it may feel natural.

Pohang[2] is not the countryside.

But it isn't Seoul either.

I lived in Pohang only for two years or so.

Still you were born and lived there.

I know but …

I sometimes can't understand what you say.

…

At the crack of dawn, my sleepiness shows.

The eyes that were plucked, dropped inside a

well.

When you are talking with other friends, what do you talk about?

What do I talk about when I am talking with my other friends?

Yes.

Well.

I'm curious.

Are you curious?

I want to understand.

Do you want to understand?

...

...

...

There was this boy who transferred to my school

when I was in the 8th grade.

And?

He was from Gangwon-do, somewhere in Gangwon-do … Well I never talked to him.

So?

One day all the boys in the class except one were called to student affairs.

Why?

They beat him.

The new student?

I heard all the boys beat him near the waste incinerator at school.

What about the one who wasn't called?

Kids from other classrooms couldn't bear to see the beating and reported it. There were many reports but no one from my classroom would talk about it. All the boys joined in, and most of the girls knew about it but clammed up, and the teacher in charge for student affairs picked one boy and offered amnesty if he would tell the truth.

You didn't know?

I didn't.

How?

Well. The last chapter of the morality textbook is about North Korea, right?

Yes.

One illustration had a picture of a kid that looked like the boy.

Ah …

After that incident I remembered it. Whenever we had morality class, the sound of giggling was heard from here and there. When boys played, they flipped coins by pogging the textbook, *ppeok ppeok, ppeok-ppeok*. One day when I had clean-up duty I went to the incinerator to throw away trash, I had to hold my nose and wince my eyes to approach it, *urghhh*, how bad did the place look? Anyway, after that thing occurred I thought that maybe, what I saw was …

Mean.

Maybe.

Of course they were mean.

Do you think so?

Do you think they did it because he deserved it?

Could they do so?

They were middle school students so they could.

Is that so?

Our school doesn't have that thing.

Are high school students different?

Sure they are different.

Are they? (Because I was born in the countryside you asked me to walk your Alaskan Malamute. Because I was born in the countryside you called me on your family's *kimjang* day[3]. Because I was born in the countryside you gave me your used shoes for my birthday gift. Because I was born in the countryside ...)

Sure they are. By the way what's your plan for this summer vacation?

At the crack of dawn, my sleepiness shows.
The eyes that were plucked, dropped inside a well.

A Santa Barbara beach, under the scorching sun in a deep blue sky, palm trees, sea lions, palm trees, pelicans, palm trees, sea otters. Sweat is transparent as a dream. A Santa Barbara beach, under the scorching sun in a deep blue sky, food trucks, chicken tacos, food trucks, sourdough sandwiches, food trucks, peach mimosas. Sweat is transparent as a dream. A Santa Barbara beach, under the scorching sun in a deep blue sky, skateboards, a red roof house, skateboards, orange wind, skateboards, light purple evening. Sweat is transparent as a dream. That feeling of summer. That emotion of a region.

I guess it was good.

It will still be the same?

That

At the crack of dawn, my sleepiness shows.
The eyes that were plucked, dropped inside a well.

You come from Pohang. What middle and high schools did you go to in Pohang?

Yes it's true I was born in Pohang, but lived there only for two years or so.

I see but why do you keep telling everyone that you are from Pohang?

Well isn't it obvious that I can't tell people that I am from Seoul?

It's a complicated problem because Seoul is densely populated.

Inside a well

Outside Seoul

California burns with wildfires.
Everything burning and burning,
Santa Barbara is shut down.
It burns and burns furiously,

works as kindling. An unexplainable feeling spreads inside me. The wind doesn't stop. I should be careful and more careful.

How?
Like how?

Inside Seoul

Outside the well

Pohang. Fires continue.
Critical. Serious.
They are extinguished. Check.

At the crack of dawn, my sleepiness shows.
The eyes that were plucked, dropped inside a well.

The beginning of the poem's epigram:
Most people completely ignore everything.
The beginning of the poem's original text:
Gae-bae.

Splat, tadpoles are in the middle of the poem

there's nothing I can do about them.
Plop, frogs are in the middle of the poem
there's nothing I can do about them.

The end of the poem
is sticky …
At the end of the poem
this pops out …

My dream is like a courthouse and each single courtroom has its own entrance.
When I go inside all the entrances are connected to one another.

Because of translation?

Why do they become clear?

Inside, outside my dream.

Translator's notes:

1 Korean word for pillow.

2 Pohang is a city in North Gyeongsang Province, South Korea.

3 A day when Korean families and neighbors gather to make enough kimchi to store and eat through the winter.

Strata

I decided to move out so bought a suitcase.

I bought a suitcase so decided to move out.

Important?

Important, I can't tell the difference between a cat's pawprints and an elephant's footprints, so I rang the doorbell.

(Waves, holding grapesorangesraspberriespistachiosasparagus, *dadakdadakhudadakpadadadak*,) (California, it's California, don't care for ya,) (putting on eel-skin bootsies) (falling on my tootsies) (perfect criticisms, I hang them from the hood of a dump truck to release them when it speeds on the bypass, I wink, at the properly vigorous sun, on a Santa Barbara sandy beach,)

(Perfectly) (deftly) the face vanished at that moment and how can I find it? I'm trying to prove what can't be proved, you tell me that I should solve the discomfort by myself,

you, so highly esteemed

will never apologize (to yawns)? I tsk-tsk (over your laziness) SMH! (over your stubbornness)

Zoo

Existing. Paying attention. Meaningful.
A humanitarian case. Just the same as.
God records and files human personalities.
Is it *che-gei* (體系)? is it *che-gei* (逮繫)?[1]

Translator's note:
1 Both Chinese characters are pronounced che-gei in Korean. The first Chinese character means a system and the second one to put someone in jail.

Statistics Korea

Flowing clouds. The blowing winds. Humans.
They all migrate.
Humans. Solitary trees. The soil.
Are they signs?
Carefully. Carefully. Eagerly.
They develop.

It's misconstrued?
Well anyway,
they all migrate.

According to Statistics Korea, in 2021, one-person households accounted for 33.4% of all households, and the percentage was predicted to reach 39.6% by 2050.[1] According to Statistics

Korea, single seniors over the age of 65 accounted for 19.5% in 2019, 19.8% in 2020, and 20.6 percent in 2021.[2] According to Statistics Korea, the inflation rate was 2.5% in 2021 and rose to 5.1% in 2022.[3] According to Statistic Korea, in 2021, 40.9% of young workers between 19 and 34 had more than two jobs and 8.5% of them more than six jobs.[4] According to Statistics Korea, the number of marriages in 2021 was 192,509 and the figure was under 200,000 for the first time since 1970.[5] According to Statistics Korea, the number of newborns in 2021 was 249,000, and the total fertility rate was 0.78.[6] According to Statistics Korea, in 2021 the ratio of suicide among teenagers to adults in their thirties was the highest ever recorded.[7] According to Statistics

Korea, in 2021, the prevalence of social isolation was 34.1%, that is, more than one of three were isolated.[8]

Are you in isolation?
That is also migration
Is it some indication?
It's developed solitude
Are you in isolation?
It has intrinsic value.
You're eagerly misconstrued
Anyway you are human
are a valued element
We'll carefully keep
reading and compiling you

Poet's notes:

1 Statistics Korea, 2022 Statistics of One-person Households (Dec. 7, 2022)

2 Statistics Korea, Population Projections for Provinces: 2020~2050 (May 27, 2022); Statistics Korea, Household Projections: 2020~2050 (June 27, 2022); The Ratio of Single Senior Citizens Aaged 65 and Over, National Indicators System (Jan 2, 2023)

3 Statistics Korea, Consumer Price Index in December 2022 (Dec. 30, 2022)

4 Statistics Korea, Statistics on Youth (Dec. 20, 2022)

5 Statistics Korea, Marriage and Divorce Statistics in 2021 (Mar. 16, 2022)

6 Statistics Korea, Preliminary Results of Birth and Death in 2022 (Feb. 21, 2023)

7 Statistics Korea, Causes of Death Statistics in 2021 (Sep. 26, 2022)

8 *Quality of Life Indicators in Korea 2021* by Shim Soo-jin and Nam Sang-min (Statistics Korea Statistics Research Institute, 2022)

Embassy

We have received an uncivil official document.

Officially, your very existence is unproven.

Unofficially, you serve to represent all the others.

But can we know what should be believed?

More UFO sightings are reported daily.

Know. You know. You know about the place. About the near distant place about the distant near place so you know about the place. Knows. The place knows. The place knows about you. About you on the verge of turning a corner about you who have turned the corner so the place knows about you. After arriving by stubbornly turning the corner you know. You know the meaning of renouncing your citizenship and the implications of exile. You know with your destiny like poems that failed to be published after being rejected over and over. You tried to show the truth that can't be shown but you know you can't give up the familiarity of your body where the soil and the grass and the roads from the place you left have taken root. So you know you can't dispense with your indispensable love. You know without denying it recklessly. You know without confirming it recklessly. *For its own security some unnamed government allows only its domestic construction companies to design and erect buildings. Some unnamed government yes that unnamed government wiretapped and spied on us.* The place knows without denying it recklessly. The place knows without confirming it recklessly. You have been penetrated. Have been penetrated as if a train has thrust through a tunnel. We know. But can we know what should be believed?

Social Worker

Everything's depressed?
Everything's hopeless.
Everything's deserved?
I submit appeals.
It's insufficient?
It's insufficient.

So, do you reuse the oil after cooking food? oh, you have a space heater? do you use it? pardon? the power went out so you use candles for light bulbs? a candlestick fell and burned your beard? no? how? was it a cigarette? why? then, open the window, I see I see, you put salt, flour too? dangerous, sure, you should dye your hair, how about wearing a hat? hard to cut off your beard, right? I'm sorry, if you don't have soap, what about perfume? people say it smells worse? important, the number of steps to your house or the height from the ground to the entrance door, the condition of wallpaper, is it okay? of course it's important, these allowances are the taxpayers' money, so you have no kids, right? yes, you can be afraid, yes, I know I know, so do you urinate well? do you mind saying that again

whether or not you can breathe,
it's impossible to breathe?

Sanatorium

A sanatorium will open where a kindergarten once was.

I was going to do an exploration in hopes of finding one.

That is so great.

Yes. That is so great.

Strange.

Strange?

Japanese has seniors' words.

Seniors' words?

They are words old people often use.

So, are they types of archaic words?

Yes. I wonder what the criteria is for "archaic."

Um, "archaic" doesn't have to mean once upon a time when tigers smoked. Words our parents use can be seniors' words.

You're right. They have their own words. I hardly use them but should learn them.

It must be hard for you to learn.

As I get older, it is. I began to learn the words with my child …

You can't keep up, right? well, me neither. Whatever it is.

Right?

Did you hear the rumor?

What rumor?

There is a flat soccer ball in every school ground.

There really is.

My child told me that.

I can't even understand the joke.

Will words we use now become seniors' words?

Eventually.

I guess so.

Strange.

Strange.

Strange.

It really is.

By the way!

What?

A sanatorium will open where a kindergarten once was.

I was going to do an exploration in hopes of finding one.

That is so great.

Yes. That is so great.

Botanical Garden

Hard to imagine. Mundane outcries. Or their exteriors.

Or a person who denies his existence despite being alive.

Or the meaning of love having been delayed. Or the chaos of it.

My heart is pulsating and I try but I cannot change my mind.

My eyes cannot be untruthful. I am watching vigilantly.

Silence bellows. I have so much to say. But I can't find the words.

Tree Burial

Radiance is all that's left

Radiance like heavy rain

I have a heap of debts

heap of radiance
a heap of radiance first sitting then sinking
heap of radiance
a heap of radiance that is always cold and warm
heap of radiance
a heap of radiance that always holds out a hand
heap of radiance
a heap of radiance that takes four seasons' hands
heap of radiance
a heap of radiance is humble in that sense

heap of radiance
a heap of radiance is brilliant as seen
heap of radiance
a heap of radiance bends its back slightly more
heap of radiance
a heap of radiance a path through sparse forest

My calves are tired
I did too much; why did I ...?
Simply because I haven't preserved your spirituality

Love and Eternity

I feel

feel like I know

The time of groups has come   The time
A group
of clouds
a group
a group of crows a group of wildebeests a group of ants a group of orcas a group of sheep a group of wolves a group of frogs a group of bees
in groups
eat when it is warm
absently
absently

Love and a Walk

For someone on an ideal walk
love will present a performance
sincerely spontaneously
casually refreshingly

So here are the lemons
growing yellow lemons
The inclines and declines
of my orchard are not

fairly flattened or flush
various things have spread

The Same as Love

Love you.

I said.

I stated.

He said he heard me.

The same? The same things?

Do. I do like. Like heaping. Mandarins heaped inside. Become concentrated. Do. I do like. Like to permeate. I permeate various places. Become concentrated. Suddenly my heart vibrates. I let it throb. Faces rotate and rotate, faces, my face, faces, your face, faces. Fresh and animated. My heartbeats, your heartbeats.

POET'S NOTE

Ah-reum-dap-seum-ni-gga?[1]

According to the National Institute of Korean Language, the etymology of the Korean word *ah-reum-dap-da* — its general definition is "beautiful"— has not yet been discovered. There are several hypotheses, but none of them has been proved, so it is hard to know the exact meaning. One hypothesis is that the suffix *eum* is added to the stem *ahl* (*ahr*) of *ahl-da* meaning "to know." Another hypothesis is inferred from *Seokbosangjeol*, a Korean biography of Gautama Buddha compiled by Prince Suyang of Joseon. It has an expression *ah-dap-da* that can be interpreted to "likely that I will do." Whichever hypothesis it is, I like it better than the current definition of "beautiful" meaning that a subject, sound, or voice is properly balanced and harmonized, so it pleases and satisfies our eyes and ears. Thinking this, I completed my second poetry book *Ah-re-um-dap-seum-ni-gga?* (Moonji Publications, 2021)

I like naming when I write poems. When I published the first book of my poems *It Is Your Turn to Understand* (Minumsa Publisher, 2019) I began to use my pen name Kwon Park instead of my real name Kwon Min-ja. I expressed the reason in my poem "A Furious Lightning Rod." With the publication of the book, I said, "When I studied women / female writers I paid attention to the women who had to use pseudonyms or male names and noticed a person's name was an important keyword in the history of women / female writers. I decided that when I write I should contemplate about what I want to write and make an effort to write what I want to write as an author, not as a female writer. That's why I decided to use my pen name Kwon Park combined with family names from my father and mother."

My second poetry book *Ah-reum-dap-seum-ni-gga?* is also about names. The Chinese character *Ja* from my first name Min-ja means a son. My parents gave me the name, accepting the traditional parental relatives' wish to have a son. They felt guilty about that later and, when my sister was born, they wanted to make a beautiful name. First, they thought to include *ah* in her first name, meaning "beautiful" in Chinese characters. But they didn't like it because it seemed to be limited to only females and sounded unreasonable. So, they decided to use *ah* in a different Chinese character that means "clean, right or correct, and graceful." Among various types of *ah-reum-dap-da* implying "clean," "right," "knowing," or "likely that I will do," which one can I, you, and we accept?

In this poetry book, *Love and the Beginning*, the history of women and the reality of female life that was the topic of my first two poetry books is expanded to all humans. I tried to understand humans by solving my questions about God's territory through love. Meanwhile, the subjects of naming became more diverse with the names of places and government agencies. Sometimes I feel difficult about the way of naming. Still, there are many parts I do not understand about naming, but *Naming and Necessity* by Saul Aaron Kripke gives me much help. The book is a hard read, but I appreciate it.

I hope my readers to be *ah-reum-dap-da*.

1 The interrogative form of *ah-reum-dap-da*.

POET'S ESSAY

Am I a poet?

The quarterly literature magazine *Literature and Society Hyphen* especially treated "Literary-Experience" in its 2022 autumn issue. They asked me to write an essay which explains with which occasions I had literary experience and what value the experiences have, even though it is difficult to explain the nature and character of "literary experience." After accepting the request, I pondered how to define "literary." After my essay entitled "Mother: How Will I write?" was published in the magazine, I continued thinking about the subject.

A definition of "literary" is "relating to, or having the characteristics of literature." The meaning of "poetic" in the dictionary is "possessing the qualities of poetry," and "fictional" means "involving prose writing formed by imagination."

"Involving" is "being engaged in something" that is not itself. That is, "literary" is related to literature, but is not literature, "poetic" involves poetry, but cannot be poetry, and "fictional" is engaged in fiction, but is not fiction. People say that a great photograph looks like a painting, and that a wonderful painting looks like a photograph. The example is a slightly different matter, but the idea lingers in my mind while defining "literary." How can I explain "it looks like something, but it is not something itself." Then, I remembered why I was interested by reading *Life As a Girl* by Tsukasa Sakaki. I agreed with the way of living and the way of loving depicted in the story, and most of all, the expression "as a girl"— the hero is a transgender woman — was clearer than "literary," "poetic," "fictional." It was familiar but unfamiliar, and unfamiliar but familiar lucidity.

Strictly speaking, "Mother: How Will I Write" is not an essay about my literary experience. In the prose, I wanted to illustrate how I had a clue about men becoming women by watching a Japanese drama entitled Mother and the identically-titled Korean movie directed by Bong Joon-ho after I discussed the topic, "Men becoming women, women becoming men, humans becoming humans" in my first two poetry books *It Is Your Turn to Understand* and *Ah-reum-dap-seum-ni-gga?*[1] At the end of my essay, I wrote "In my next poetry book, I plan to expand the idea of human becoming humans. That is also about me becoming a human. Will I marry? This question accompanies consecutive questions. Can I love someone? Can I be a mother? I don't know. But I can't leave these questions unsolved. Whichever the answers are, I want to come to some conclusion." I decided to give the title *Love and the Beginning* to my third poetry book. And I found some clues to answer my questions about the natures and characteristics of "literary," "poetic," and "fictional" through my poem "Most People" in my third poetry book.

Some of my readers will wonder why I was so serious about the meaning of "literary experience." After publishing *It Is Your Turn to Understand*, I was asked several questions. The first question was about my love stories and marriage plans, and the second one was how I could drastically change my literary style compared to my earlier poems. They also made comments that *It Is Your Turn to Understand* is like fiction, prose, a thesis, an article. I thought I could answer them by writing more poems and wondered if my second poetry book *Ah-reum-dap-seum-ni-gga?* answered those questions to some extent. Then I thought my third poetry book should answer unsolved parts of the questions. Through my poems, can I answer the question about what poetry is? Am I a poet? What kind of a poet am I? While being immersed in the thoughts, I got the request from the magazine publisher and had to figure out the meanings of words "literary," "poetic" and "fictional." I wonder how much this book has solved my concerns.

Using specific and long footnotes is one of the representative features of my earlier poetry books, but in this book, I added only a couple of brief footnotes and increased the frequency of using epigraphs, which is another feature of my poetry.

I explained my footnotes in literatary magazines and a podcast. I used footnotes to complement the limitations that the genre of literature has, and they functioned as another consciousness, unconsciousness, and for borrowing and rephrasing, not just as simply informative references. In the poem "Pohang+Jamsil+Yeouido.hwp→jpg" from *Ah-reum-dap-seum-ni-gga?* I narrated, "Questions edited the actual interview. The answer below is a response from another consciousness. It is part of infinite consciousness." I have explained my poems, saying, "they are processed with epigraphs," "they are processed with original texts," or "they are processed with footnotes." I, however, wonder if my explanation is persuasive for literary circles and readers. I also wonder if my experiments conducted in *Love and the Beginning* will be successful.

Seemingly I leave even more questions, but I think writing poetry does not suggest answers to questions but rather the procedure of seeking answers. In that sense, *Love and the Beginning* is clear. In the next poetry book, can I arrive at a love I haven't figured out?

1 Refer to "Poet's Note" in this book.

COMMENTARY

K

POET

A Formalist Dreaming Freedom

Kim Joo-won (Literary critic)

Kwon Park has a lot to say through her poetry. She often employs multiple footnotes as she tries to supplement and support her poems. Her footnotes originate from official reports or academic theses, and she adopts them as her own poetic methodology. Footnotes may be seen as unpoetic, but she uses them as a way to disclose poetic truths rather than to prove objective facts. This truth is more honest than conventional wisdom or facts. The voices in her poems disclose their experiences and emotions without reservation. Frank with herself and honest with others, she expresses the complications of "understanding" (*It Is Your Turn to Understand*) and "beauty" (*Ah-reum-*

dap-seum-ni-gga?) and flings questions about the contradictions and truths concealed in those concepts.

She presents good poems that are accompanied by fresh formalities. Unlike her earlier books, *Love and the Beginning* has few footnotes, but is still filled with various experiments. Readers perceive form before appreciating content. Many lines have a regular number of syllables, and conventional rules of punctuation and grammar are ignored. The form of modern poetry rooted in free verse is liberal; separating stanzas or lines are arbitrary actions. However, Kwon applies her own rules. Refer again to her footnotes. In modern poetry, footnotes function only as references and do not have standardized forms; Kwon's unpoetic footnotes play active roles to create meaning in the forms of her refined verse.

Poems in *Love and the Beginning* follow regular rules and forms, but poetic meaning is easily accomplished. In "Most People," for example, the lines "At the crack of dawn, my sleepiness shows. / The eyes that were plucked, dropped inside a well," and "Inside a well / Outside Seoul" are equal in syllable count. This poem describes how common it is that most people bully weaker people in daily life. The voice of this poem is considered a country person, since she was born in a minor city (Pohang) and knows the dialectic term for "dawn." Due to prejudice, she is criticized for not understanding well what other people say. This poem introduces a more serious episode when the speaker's companion tells the story of a junior high school boy who was bullied by classmates. There was no special reason. The bullied boy was from another region and looked like a North Korean boy shown in a textbook. The companion regards the incident as a simple event and believes these things don't happen at her high school.

This poem reveals how casually we insult and stigmatize others. “Most people” sometimes have violent thoughts toward minorities, and certain geographical locations or cultural groups become excuses to justify discrimination which is “most people’s” automatic reaction. In another example, the typical image of “A Santa Barbara beach” is an attractive destination with beautiful scenery. It is a cliché, like “That feeling of summer. That emotion of a region.” The feelings of people in trouble are expressed in relation to their birthplace. When we hear the names of such places, “An unexplainable feeling spreads inside” our minds and we cannot understand the feeling’s origin. This is why we should be careful. Those feelings “work as kindling” and “The wind doesn’t stop,” so wildfires can be the result.

Repetitive phrases with linguistic play like “The eyes that were plucked, dropped inside a well,” and “Inside a well / Outside Seoul” are meaningful. Plucked eyes is a metaphor of stigmatization, as individual's features are altered based on social norms. When the eyes are removed, blindness leads to isolation like being "inside a well." "Inside a well / Outside Seoul" is nonexistent; "Gaebae," the dialectic term for dawn, is disregarded because "Most people completely ignore everything." Settings such as a zoo, the Statistics Korea website, an embassy and a sanatorium represent forms that define our lives. These places, like "A Santa Barbara beach," are confined in our typical perception.

Demographic statistics about one-person households, inflation rates, employment, marriage, etc. appear in "Statistics Korea." The numerical data based on this research is not material for pleasant reading, but is the data completely unrelated to our lives? This poem reads an individual's "developed solitude," "migration," "isolation" and "intrinsic value" embedded in statistics. "Anyway you are human / are a valued element," but perhaps "You're eagerly misconstrued." In the poem, statistics are the objective material that manifest people's loneliness, love, or pain. The speakers in Kwon's poems draw deeply personal emotions from the familiar public agencies. The poem "Embassy" maintains a dual image of official and unofficial representations. An embassy supervises one's citizenship or exile, denial or confirmation, personal privacy or wiretapping. It is even involved in people's fates, their sense of national identity, even their love lives. An embassy is where various inner actions occur. Referring to the affairs of an embassy, "We know. But can we know what should be believed?" Kwon is excellent at discovering poetic truths in unpoetic objects, constructing relationships between individuals and society that go beyond the common dichotomy.

Kwon's poems in *Love and the Beginning* appear

as gatherings of different-sized boxes in regular patterns. These are modern poems that remind us of *sijo* or *haiku*. It is reminiscent of the French OuLipo experimental writers creating works with constraints and rules in the 1960s. They dismantled and reassembled words, sentences, or the alphabet. They wrote without punctuation, and their fixed verses were variously applied. Forms and rules were not boring. They called themselves "rats who build the labyrinth from which they will try to escape." (Raymond Queneau) This motto contains their esthetic desire with which they sought to enjoy maximum freedom in extreme constraints. It is similar to *haiku* that seeks spiritual freedom within strict rules. Kwon Park creates this philosophy within the Korean language. Unfortunately, if her poems are translated, the unique beauty of the Korean form will disappear. She is a formalist finding a path by her own rules. Imagine solving a Rubik's Cube. In her poems, rules and form are playful. Surprisingly, we meet new freedoms in constraints. In collective representations that define our lives, we can face a new self not yet recognized and enjoy freedom that is not confined by established perceptions and names.

Kwon Park's poems appear in the distance. Places, footnotes, regularity and restrictions are unfamiliar. Her poems break from conventional concepts and perceptions through extreme experiments. If Yi Sang were alive today, wouldn't he write poems like hers? No one recognized him then, are we not recognizing her now? In Poet's Essay of this book, she immerses herself in terms of "literary" and "poetic." A poem is good when it has not only fresh content, but fresh forms. Kwon Park's poetry is already literary and poetic enough.

to her. Described as a "library poet," she says her poetry is an unfamiliar bridgehead built between academia and creativity, and she uses her poems as encyclopedic windows and doors. Actually, however, her assertions seem like phenomena to realize her absent legitimacy. In short, she strongly asserts the radical expression of literature's failure to show she is extremely ethical toward literature that has failed or will fail. As a maverick in literary circles, her statement challenges existing literature and is also an intensive inquiry for an eager desire for an alternative literature. The fundamental intention of the word "failure" is, as she once said, "to organize failed methods and show direction." She seeks to heighten the expectations for this new literature and the poetic desire to search for new methodology.

Jeon Hae-soo (poet and critic)

K-POET
Love and the Beginning

Written by Kwon Park
Translated by YoungShil Ji, Daniel T. Parker
Published by ASIA Publishers
Address 445, Hoedong-gil, Paju-si, Gyeonggi-do, Korea
(Seoul Office: 161-1, Seodal-ro, Dongjak-gu, Seoul, Korea)
Tel (822).3280.5058
Email bookasia@hanmail.net
Homepage Address www.bookasia.org

ISBN 979-11-5662-317-5 (set) | 979-11-5662-644-2 (04810)
First published in Korea by ASIA Publishers 2023

This book is published with the support of the Literature Translation Institute of Korea (LTI Korea).

바이링궐 에디션 한국 대표 소설

한국문학의 가장 중요하고 첨예한 문제의식을 가진 작가들의 대표작을 주제별로 선정!
하버드 한국학 연구원 및 세계 각국의 한국문학 전문 번역진이 참여한 번역 시리즈!
미국 하버드대학교와 컬럼비아대학교 동아시아학과, 캐나다 브리티시컬럼비아대학교 아시아학과 등 해외 대학에서 교재로 채택!

바이링궐 에디션 한국 대표 소설 set 1

분단 Division

01 병신과 머저리-**이청준** The Wounded-**Yi Cheong-jun**
02 어둠의 혼-**김원일** Soul of Darkness-**Kim Won-il**
03 순이삼촌-**현기영** Sun-i Samch'on-**Hyun Ki-young**
04 엄마의 말뚝 1-**박완서** Mother's Stake I-**Park Wan-suh**
05 유형의 땅-**조정래** The Land of the Banished-**Jo Jung-rae**

산업화 Industrialization

06 무진기행-**김승옥** Record of a Journey to Mujin-**Kim Seung-ok**
07 삼포 가는 길-**황석영** The Road to Sampo-**Hwang Sok-yong**
08 아홉 켤레의 구두로 남은 사내-**윤흥길** The Man Who Was Left as Nine Pairs of Shoes-**Yun Heung-gil**
09 돌아온 우리의 친구-**신상웅** Our Friend's Homecoming-**Shin Sang-ung**
10 원미동 시인-**양귀자** The Poet of Wŏnmi-dong-**Yang Kwi-ja**

여성 Women

11 중국인 거리-**오정희** Chinatown-**Oh Jung-hee**
12 풍금이 있던 자리-**신경숙** The Place Where the Harmonium Was-**Shin Kyung-sook**
13 하나코는 없다-**최윤** The Last of Hanak'o-**Ch'oe Yun**
14 인간에 대한 예의-**공지영** Human Decency-**Gong Ji-young**
15 빈처-**은희경** Poor Man's Wife-**Eun Hee-kyung**

바이링궐 에디션 한국 대표 소설 set 2

자유 Liberty

16 필론의 돼지-**이문열** Pilon's Pig-**Yi Mun-yol**
17 슬로우 불릿-**이대환** Slow Bullet-**Lee Dae-hwan**
18 직선과 독가스-**임철우** Straight Lines and Poison Gas-**Lim Chul-woo**
19 깃발-**홍희담** The Flag-**Hong Hee-dam**
20 새벽 출정-**방현석** Off to Battle at Dawn-**Bang Hyeon-seok**

사랑과 연애 Love and Love Affairs

21 별을 사랑하는 마음으로-**윤후명** With the Love for the Stars-**Yun Hu-myong**
22 목련공원-**이승우** Magnolia Park-**Lee Seung-u**
23 칼에 찔린 자국-**김인숙** Stab-**Kim In-suk**
24 회복하는 인간-**한강** Convalescence-**Han Kang**
25 트렁크-**정이현** In the Trunk-**Jeong Yi-hyun**

남과 북 South and North

26 판문점-**이호철** Panmunjom-**Yi Ho-chol**
27 수난 이대-**하근찬** The Suffering of Two Generations-**Ha Geun-chan**
28 분지-**남정현** Land of Excrement-**Nam Jung-hyun**
29 봄 실상사-**정도상** Spring at Silsangsa Temple-**Jeong Do-sang**
30 은행나무 사랑-**김하기** Gingko Love-**Kim Ha-kee**

바이링궐 에디션 한국 대표 소설 set 3

서울 Seoul

31 눈사람 속의 검은 항아리-**김소진** The Dark Jar within the Snowman-**Kim So-jin**
32 오후, 가로지르다-**하성란** Traversing Afternoon-**Ha Seong-nan**
33 나는 봉천동에 산다-**조경란** I Live in Bongcheon-dong-**Jo Kyung-ran**
34 그렇습니까? 기린입니다-**박민규** Is That So? I'm A Giraffe-**Park Min-gyu**
35 성탄특선-**김애란** Christmas Specials-**Kim Ae-ran**

전통 Tradition

36 무자년의 가을 사흘-**서정인** Three Days of Autumn, 1948-**Su Jung-in**
37 유자소전-**이문구** A Brief Biography of Yuja-**Yi Mun-gu**
38 향기로운 우물 이야기-**박범신** The Fragrant Well-**Park Bum-shin**
39 월행-**송기원** A Journey under the Moonlight-**Song Ki-won**
40 협죽도 그늘 아래-**성석제** In the Shade of the Oleander-**Song Sok-ze**

아방가르드 Avant-garde

41 아겔다마-**박상륭** Akeldama-**Park Sang-ryoong**
42 내 영혼의 우물-**최인석** A Well in My Soul-**Choi In-seok**
43 당신에 대해서-**이인성** On You-**Yi In-seong**
44 회색 時-**배수아** Time In Gray-**Bae Su-ah**
45 브라운 부인-**정영문** Mrs. Brown-**Jung Young-moon**

바이링궐 에디션 한국 대표 소설 set 4

디아스포라 Diaspora

46 속옷-**김남일** Underwear-**Kim Nam-il**
47 상하이에 두고 온 사람들-**공선옥** People I Left in Shanghai-**Gong Sun-ok**
48 모두에게 복된 새해-**김연수** Happy New Year to Everyone-**Kim Yeon-su**
49 코끼리-**김재영** The Elephant-**Kim Jae-young**
50 먼지별-**이경** Dust Star-**Lee Kyung**

가족 Family

51 혜자의 눈꽃-**천승세** Hye-ja's Snow-Flowers-**Chun Seung-sei**
52 아베의 가족-**전상국** Ahbe's Family-**Jeon Sang-guk**
53 문 앞에서-**이동하** Outside the Door-**Lee Dong-ha**
54 그리고, 축제-**이혜경** And Then the Festival-**Lee Hye-kyung**
55 봄밤-**권여선** Spring Night-**Kwon Yeo-sun**

유머 Humor

56 오늘의 운세-**한창훈** Today's Fortune-**Han Chang-hoon**
57 새-**전성태** Bird-**Jeon Sung-tae**
58 밀수록 다시 가까워지는-**이기호** So Far, and Yet So Near-**Lee Ki-ho**
59 유리방패-**김중혁** The Glass Shield-**Kim Jung-hyuk**
60 전당포를 찾아서-**김종광** The Pawnshop Chase-**Kim Chong-kwang**

바이링궐 에디션 한국 대표 소설 set 5

관계 Relationship

61 도둑견습 – **김주영** Robbery Training-**Kim Joo-young**
62 사랑하라, 희망 없이 – **윤영수** Love, Hopelessly-**Yun Young-su**
63 봄날 오후, 과부 셋 – **정지아** Spring Afternoon, Three Widows-**Jeong Ji-a**
64 유턴 지점에 보물지도를 묻다 - **윤성희** Burying a Treasure Map at the U-turn-**Yoon Sung-hee**
65 쁘이거나 쯔이거나 - **백가흠** Puy, Thuy, Whatever-**Paik Ga-huim**

일상의 발견 Discovering Everyday Life

66 나는 음식이다 – **오수연** I Am Food-**Oh Soo-yeon**
67 트럭 – **강영숙** Truck-**Kang Young-sook**
68 통조림 공장 - **편혜영** The Canning Factory-**Pyun Hye-young**
69 꽃 – **부희령** Flowers-**Pu Hee-ryoung**
70 피의일요일 – **윤이형** BloodySunday-**Yun I-hyeong**

금기와 욕망 Taboo and Desire

71 북소리 - **송영** Drumbeat-**Song Yong**
72 발칸의 장미를 내게 주었네 - **정미경** He Gave Me Roses of the Balkans-**Jung Mi-kyung**
73 아무도 돌아오지 않는 밤 - **김숨** The Night Nobody Returns Home-**Kim Soom**
74 젓가락여자 - **천운영** Chopstick Woman-**Cheon Un-yeong**
75 아직 일어나지 않은 일 - **김미월** What Has Yet to Happen-**Kim Mi-wol**

바이링궐 에디션 한국 대표 소설 set 6

운명 Fate

76 언니를 놓치다 - **이경자** Losing a Sister-**Lee Kyung-ja**
77 아들 - **윤정모** Father and Son-**Yoon Jung-mo**
78 명두 - **구효서** Relics-**Ku Hyo-seo**
79 모독 - **조세희** Insult-**Cho Se-hui**
80 화요일의 강 - **손홍규** Tuesday River-**Son Hong-gyu**

미의 사제들 Aesthetic Priests

81 고수 - **이외수** Grand Master-**Lee Oisoo**
82 말을 찾아서 - **이순원** Looking for a Horse-**Lee Soon-won**
83 상춘곡 - **윤대녕** Song of Everlasting Spring-**Youn Dae-nyeong**
84 삭매와 자미 - **김별아** Sakmae and Jami-**Kim Byeol-ah**
85 저만치 혼자서 - **김훈** Alone Over There-**Kim Hoon**

식민지의 벌거벗은 자들 The Naked in the Colony

86 감자 - **김동인** Potatoes-**Kim Tong-in**
87 운수 좋은 날 - **현진건** A Lucky Day-**Hyŏn Chin'gŏn**
88 탈출기 - **최서해** Escape-**Ch'oe So-hae**
89 과도기 - **한설야** Transition-**Han Seol-ya**
90 지하촌 - **강경애** The Underground Village-**Kang Kyŏng-ae**

바이링궐 에디션 한국 대표 소설 set 7

백치가 된 식민지 지식인 Colonial Intellectuals Turned "Idiots"

91 날개 - **이상** Wings-**Yi Sang**
92 김 강사와 T 교수 - **유진오** Lecturer Kim and Professor T-**Chin-O Yu**
93 소설가 구보씨의 일일 - **박태원** A Day in the Life of Kubo the Novelist-**Pak Taewon**
94 비 오는 길 - **최명익** Walking in the Rain-**Ch'oe Myŏngik**
95 빛 속에 - **김사량** Into the Light-**Kim Sa-ryang**

한국의 잃어버린 얼굴 Traditional Korea's Lost Faces

96 봄·봄 – **김유정** Spring, Spring–**Kim Yu-jeong**
97 벙어리 삼룡이 – **나도향** Samnyong the Mute–**Na Tohyang**
98 달밤 – **이태준** An Idiot's Delight–**Yi T'ae-jun**
99 사랑손님과 어머니 – **주요섭** Mama and the Boarder–**Chu Yo-sup**
100 갯마을 – **오영수** Seaside Village–**Oh Yeongsu**

해방 전후(前後) Before and After Liberation

101 소망 – **채만식** Juvesenility–**Ch'ae Man-Sik**
102 두 파산 – **염상섭** Two Bankruptcies–**Yom Sang-Seop**
103 풀잎 – **이효석** Leaves of Grass–**Lee Hyo-seok**
104 맥 – **김남천** Barley–**Kim Namch'on**
105 꺼삐딴 리 – **전광용** Kapitan Ri–**Chŏn Kwangyong**

전후(戰後) Korea After the Korean War

106 소나기 – **황순원** The Cloudburst–**Hwang Sun-Won**
107 등신불 – **김동리** Tŭngsin-bul–**Kim Tong-ni**
108 요한 시집 – **장용학** The Poetry of John–**Chang Yong-hak**
109 비 오는 날 – **손창섭** Rainy Days–**Son Chang-sop**
110 오발탄 – **이범선** A Stray Bullet–**Lee Beomseon**

K-픽션 시리즈 | Korean Fiction Series

〈K-픽션〉 시리즈는 한국문학의 젊은 상상력입니다. 최근 발표된 가장 우수하고 흥미로운 작품을 엄선하여 출간하는 〈K-픽션〉은 한국문학의 생생한 현장을 국내외 독자들과 실시간으로 공유하고자 기획되었습니다. 〈바이링궐 에디션 한국 대표 소설〉 시리즈를 통해 검증된 탁월한 번역진이 참여하여 원작의 재미와 품격을 최대한 살린 〈K-픽션〉 시리즈는 매 계절마다 새로운 작품을 선보입니다.

001 버핏과의 저녁 식사-**박민규** Dinner with Buffett-**Park Min-gyu**

002 아르판-**박형서** Arpan-**Park hyoung su**

003 애드벌룬-**손보미** Hot Air Balloon-**Son Bo-mi**

004 나의 클린트 이스트우드-**오한기** My Clint Eastwood-**Oh Han-ki**

005 이베리아의 전갈-**최민우** Dishonored-**Choi Min-woo**

006 양의 미래-**황정은** Kong's Garden-**Hwang Jung-eun**

007 대니-**윤이형** Danny-**Yun I-hyeong**

008 퇴근-**천명관** Homecoming-**Cheon Myeong-kwan**

009 옥화-**금희** Ok-hwa-**Geum Hee**

010 시차-**백수린** Time Difference-**Baik Sou linne**

011 올드 맨 리버-**이장욱** Old Man River-**Lee Jang-wook**

012 권순찬과 착한 사람들-**이기호** Kwon Sun-chan and Nice People-**Lee Ki-ho**

013 알바생 자르기-**장강명** Fired-**Chang Kang-myoung**

014 어디로 가고 싶으신가요-**김애란** Where Would You Like To Go?-**Kim Ae-ran**

015 세상에서 가장 비싼 소설-**김민정** The World's Most Expensive Novel-**Kim Min-jung**

016 체스의 모든 것-**김금희** Everything About Chess-**Kim Keum-hee**

017 할로윈-**정한아** Halloween-**Chung Han-ah**

018 그 여름-**최은영** The Summer-**Choi Eunyoung**

019 어느 피씨주의자의 종생기-**구병모** The Story of P.C.-**Gu Byeong-mo**

020 모르는 영역-**권여선** An Unknown Realm-**Kwon Yeo-sun**

021 4월의 눈-**손원평** April Snow-**Sohn Won-pyung**

022 서우-**강화길** Seo-u-**Kang Hwa-gil**

023 가출-**조남주** Run Away-**Cho Nam-joo**

024 연애의 감정학-**백영옥** How to Break Up Like a Winner-**Baek Young-ok**

025 창모-**우다영** Chang-mo-**Woo Da-young**

026 검은 방-**정지아** The Black Room-**Jeong Ji-a**

027 도쿄의 마야-**장류진** Maya in Tokyo-**Jang Ryu-jin**

028 홀리데이 홈-**편혜영** Holiday Home-**Pyun Hye-young**

029 해피 투게더-**서장원** Happy Together-**Seo Jang-won**

030 골드러시-**서수진** Gold Rush-**Seo Su-jin**

031 당신이 보고 싶어하는 세상-**장강명** The World You Want to See-**Chang Kang-myoung**

032 지난밤 내 꿈에-**정한아** Last Night, In My Dream-**Chung Han-ah**

Special 휴가중인 시체-**김중혁** Corpse on Vacation-**Kim Jung-hyuk**

Special 사파에서-**방현석** Love in Sa Pa-**Bang Hyeon-seok**